Contents:

First published in 2005 by The School of Emotional Literacy

This edition published in 2008 by Speechmark Publishing Ltd,
70 Alston Drive, Bradwell Abbey, Milton Keynes MK13 9HG
Tel: +44 (0) 1908 326944   Fax: +44 (0) 1908 326960

www.speechmark.net
www.schoolofemotional-literacy.com

British Library Cataloguing in Publication Data
A catalogue record for this book is available from the British Library

002-5540 / Printed in the United Kingdom / 3080

ISBN: 978 086388 738 3

1 INTRODUCTION TO MULTIPLE INTELLIGENCES

WHAT IS IT?

Multiple Intelligence theory is a new way of thinking about the intelligence a child exhibits.   This way we don't ask ourselves 'How intelligent is that child?' instead we say 'In what ways is that child intelligent?'

This seems to be a time of change, where we are exchanging old paradigms, or ways of thinking, for new ones. There are many implications underlying these new paradigms, which mean that we have to examine our current practice – and often change that too. For example, here are some old paradigms about intelligence compared to some new ones. In the assessment section of this book you will find some more new paradigms about the assessment process too.

Old and new paradigms about intelligence

New paradigm:	•	Intelligence is not fixed or static at birth
Old paradigm:	•	Intelligence was more or less determined by heredity
	•	Intelligence can be assessed through tests yielding a quantifiable intelligence quotient (IQ)
New paradigm	•	Intelligence is influenced by many factors - environmental, cultural and socialisation
Old paradigm:	•	We are born with an unchangeable intellectual capacity
New paradigm	•	Intelligence is a set of capabilities that are continually expanding and changing throughout one's life!

The old way of thinking about 'how clever' someone is has been to give them a pen and paper test that checks their ability to read, calculate, make deductions and form categories. If a child is not particularly strong in these aspects they will score low on the traditional IQ test and this is likely to affect the rest of their schooling.

This can be as subtle as influencing the way their teachers or parents perceive them and thus what they inspire a child to achieve (or not), to as direct as being put into special classes depending on the results.   Of course the perception that a child forms of themselves is just as influential – positively or negatively – and impacts greatly on their performance. This more traditional form of assessment misses a great deal of what is valuable, unique and rich within a child and takes no account of the wide variety of ways in which someone can express and demonstrate their 'cleverness'.

We all know children who do not shine in the traditional academic subjects but who are popular, kind, and wonderful at being mentors to younger children. How can that intelligence and ability be assessed and valued with the IQ tests available today? Even with ongoing assessment of work and reports from teachers about the social and emotional development of pupils the unique mosaic of a child's ability are not captured well within the systems we currently use.

HISTORY

Dr Howard Gardner, a Professor of Education at Harvard University with particular interest in developmental psychology, developed this theory of Intelligence and published it in his book, Frames of Mind in 1983. Since his initial careful formulation of his theory of Multiple Intelligences his work has inspired many gifted educators to work with the theory in their classrooms, schools, homes or special educational settings. It has been one of the most influential theories of the 20th Century and looks set to continue its influence into the 21st. His theory set out the existence of 7 intelligences and challenged the more static previous view of intelligence.

When Dr Gardner began his work, and certainly when he published his book, he had not anticipated the extent to which people still thought of intelligence as one thing, a general capacity that everyone has to some greater or lesser degree. It has been my experience that this assumption still prevails here in the UK today. This common assumption about Intelligence has meant that we think of it as something that we can measure by using paper and pencil tests and that measure will remain constant throughout life, changing only in old age or through organic causes, such as early dementia or a tumour, when we may lose some of our cognitive powers.

However, taking a moment to think about the ways in which we can express our ability to understand the world and create artefacts that have value within our own cultural contexts quickly shows that we have far more complex abilities than can be captured by a test that assesses ones ability to read, write and manipulate shapes, patterns and figures. Using Dr Gardner's own example of a Parisian composer seated at her microcomputer preparing to compose a new piece of music we can see that intelligence has stretched far beyond those simple concepts. However it also begins to pose the problem of how this kind, or these kinds, of intelligence can be assessed.

A WIDER VIEW OF INTELLIGENCE

Dr Gardner brought a much wider view of Intelligence to us. He needed his definition to encompass many more universal competencies than had been thought of before. Thus his definition of intelligence is: the ability to solve problems or create products that is valued in one or more cultural settings. He then went on to establish a set of criteria by which intelligence could be verified. If it fitted each, particularly with regard to the biological and anthropological evidence, then it would be included in his Multiple Intelligences. This explains the fairly recent addition of an eighth intelligence, Naturalist, to his original seven.

Here is a selection from his 8 criteria against which any potential intelligence can be assessed:

Each intelligence is capable of being symbolised.

This means that as humans we have the ability to convey our ideas and experiences through 'symbols' such as words, pictures or numbers. Thus the spatially intelligent person is able to convey and express their ideas through symbol such as pictures and in turn will understand the world more readily if it is symbolised this way for them.

Each intelligence has its own developmental history

There are times during maturation when certain abilities or potential ability can blossom more readily than at other times. Musical ability for instance is the earliest to have a window of opportunity open for it to be developed and flourish and this ability can continue to develop and be used creatively well into old age.

On the other hand logical mathematical ability has a different looking developmental trend. Its window of opportunity opens later than the musical one and develops slowly peaking in late adolescence or early twenties then declines in later life.

Each intelligence is vulnerable if different specific parts of the brain receive an injury.

An example of this would be someone whos frontal lobes of the left hemisphere of the cortex where linguistic processing takes place, have been damaged. This person could nevertheless still sing, draw and dance without any difficulty.

Each intelligence can produce products that are valued by the culture the person exists within

This is where the theory of multiple intelligences differs from the more traditional view of paper and pencil assessment of intelligence. The MI theorists suggest looking to man's accomplishments rather than test scores to see intelligence in action. An IQ test may ask someone to develop a sequence of numbers backwards – an MI assessor would be more interested in studying a work of art produced by a certain culture as an example of intelligence.

The existence of idiots, savants, prodigies and other exceptional individuals
In this case, rather similar to the last, Dr Gardner argued that we can learn a lot about each intelligence and its relative autonomy from the others. This can be done by investigating the lives and abilities of people such as the idiot savant Raymond, a real life person brought to the general public by Dustin Hoffman's superb performance in the film of Raymond's life The Rainman. This man was able to compute figures and statistical information in a fraction of a second but had very poor linguistic, interpersonal or intrapersonal abilities.

An evolutionary history
In this criteria the intelligence is investigated for its relevance and presence in the early history of mankind and also in our closest animal cousins, the primates and beyond to other life forms.

Primitive cave art clearly shows evidence of spatial intelligence, a sense of self through their depiction of themselves, naturalist intelligence through the close observation of animal forms etc. Interpersonal intelligence is seen in primates and other species when the evidence of communal living groups and maternal bonding is investigated.

Support from psychometric findings
Although a strong antagonist of standardised psychometric tests such as the IQ test, ironically they can be used to support the MI theory since people can easily have far higher scores in one section – such as the linguistic vocabulary sub test rather than in the arithmetic and number oriented part. Problems arise with these criteria since standardised tests do not encompass the other areas postulated by Dr Gardner so using this method to support the relative autonomy of all of the intelligences does not work. Nevertheless it does offer some support for certain intelligences.

2 THE 8 INTELLIGENCES

Here is an outline of each of the eight intelligences currently postulated by Howard Gardner. Some others claim that there are many more than eight intelligences. The most famous of these others is Danah Zohar and the spiritual intelligence. Gardner does not deny that there could well be other intelligences, some people even going so far as to say there could be hundreds. However what he does say is that the number of defined intelligences will depend on the set of criteria set up to establish their credentials. In his case he has set up criteria and the other intelligences, such as spiritual, do not fit all of the criteria in his theory. Thus they may not join his framework and be listed as one or more of the intelligences in his list. This does not mean that given a different and well constructed set of criteria they could not exist in another list and be thought of as a valid intelligence.

This section gives you a description of the intelligence, an example of a person with it showing strongly and ways to recognise this strength in others. As you go through it think of yourself first. What ones do you have a natural affinity with? Once you have done this for yourself it should be easier to begin doing the same for your children, pupils, friends etc.

WHAT THEY ARE

1 Linguistic

2 Logical mathematical

3 Spatial

4 Musical

5 Bodily – Kinaesthetic

6 Intrapersonal

7 Interpersonal

8 Naturalist

LINGUISTIC

This intelligence helps us understand the relationship between words, grammar, meanings and communication of all forms. People who are strong in this can show it through their capacity to understand other languages, or through being able to write fluently or present to audiences easily.

Examples of roles where this intelligence is strong:
an orator, stand-up comedian, author, translator.

Everyday examples:
reading, writing, sending emails...

Recognising it:
Loves reading and listening
Writes
Likes the history of words
Enjoys seeing the connection between words
Thinks in stories not sequences
Likes to talk and present

LOGICAL MATHEMATICAL

This means that you can work well with numbers and enjoy the symmetry of logic and reasoning disciplines. It means being able to understand the relationships between numbers, patterns, forms etc to see sequences and causal connections.

Examples of roles where this intelligence is strong;
scientists, mathematicians, actuaries.

Everyday examples:
Balance cheque books, follow a train timetable, reading financial or science reports in the papers.

Recognising it:
Does things methodically
Logical
Organised
Precise
Measures things
Puts things in sequence
Practical

SPATIAL

This intelligence means that you can visualise things in your mind's eye. It helps you make relationships and understand the balances between objects and space. It helps you create things in 3 dimensions.

Examples of roles where this intelligence is strong:
artist, sculptor, architect.

Everyday examples:
redecorating our home, appreciating a work of art in a museum, planning the garden.

Recognising it:
Describes things in a lot of detail
Uses graphics to organise
Dreams in colour and has vivid imagination
Learns through images, pictures and symbols
Likes to have a model
Uses maps rather than directions
Remembers pictures rather than words

MUSICAL

This involves being able to understand and follow the relationships between sounds and rhythms and between sounds and silence. This intelligence picks up on the overt or covert music in the noise around them.

Examples of roles where this intelligence is strong:
diva, DJ, piano tuner.

Everyday examples:
enjoy some music on the radio, listening to someone speak who has a beautifully modulated voice.

Recognising it:
Good listener
Likes to hear rather than see
Distracted by sounds
Relates to concepts when presented in music or rhythm patterns
Remembers lyrics easily

BODILY - KINAESTHETIC

This is the intelligence of the whole body. The person who can feel and understand (usually unconsciously) the relationships between their muscles, tendons, strength, energy, space, the ground and skeleton and make the best use of it all. They are best at learning when they are doing. They can have the intelligence of their whole bodies (athlete) or specifically their hands (seamstress).

Examples of roles where this intelligence is strong;
athletes, car mechanics, actors.

Everyday examples:
dancing, unscrewing jars, walking and running around!

Recognising it
Does lots of things
Is active
Dramatic
Likes to learn by doing the task not hearing about it
Likes variety
Makes things

INTRAPERSONAL

The ability to understand oneself and know who and what you are. It means that you know what you are or aren't good at and what you like or dislike. The self-reflective person will think of their life goals and purpose, finding ways to make that real in their everyday life.

Examples of roles where this intelligence is strong:
entrepreneurs, therapists, cousellors.

Everyday examples:
taking some quiet time to think about your day.

Recognising it:

Likes working alone	Self-aware
One or two close friends	Likes to go last
Analytical	Likes quiet thinking time
Independent	

INTERPERSONAL

This intelligence involves being able to understand the relationships between yourself and other people and between others who you may be observing or hearing about. It involves being able to feel empathic, to being able to influence and persuade groups. It means that you can tune in and read people's signs and size a person up quickly.

Examples of roles where this intelligence is strong:
interviewers, team leaders, mediators.

Everyday examples:
talking with friends, knowing when there is tension between two people.

Recognising it:

Likes learning in groups	Wants feedback
Communicates	Has friends
Cooperates	Thinks aloud
Talks a lot	Sensitive
Remembers characters and stories	

NATURALIST

This involves being able to make relationships between aspects of the natural world. People strong in this intelligence are very aware of the impact of an event on an ecosystem. For example, recently the Foot and Mouth disease outbreak made large differences to the ecosystems in the fields of Britain. Ramblers and cattle were not in them at the usual times of year and for instance, bird activity patterns changed. People living in these environments noticed this while others, less strong on this intelligence, didn't.

Examples of roles where this intelligence is strong:
Veterinarians, ecologists, farmers.

Everyday examples:
appreciating the scent of some roses, noticing signs of the change in season, being aware of the typical behaviour of the household pet.

Recognising it:
Relates well to pets
Takes actions to conserve resources
Keeps records or collects natural phenomena
Does well in subjects that deal with living systems

3 ASSESSING MULTIPLE INTELLIGENCES

The new paradigms about intelligence have also brought our thinking round to how we might go about assessing such a multi-stranded concept. This in turn has opened up our thinking about the paradigms we have been used to working with – and articulating the new ones. Here is a summary of the old and new in relation to assessment.

The Old Assessment Paradigm	The New Assessment Paradigm
All students are basically the same and learn in the same way; therefore, instruction and testing can be standardised.	There are no standard students. Each is unique; therefore instruction and testing must be individualised and varied.
Norm- or criterion-referenced standardised test scores are the main and most accurate indicators of student knowledge and learning.	Performance based, direct assessment, involving a variety of testing instruments, gives a more complete, accurate, and fair picture of student knowledge and learning.
Paper-and-pencil tests are the only valid way to assess academic progress.	Student created and maintained portfolios, which include paper and pencil tests as well as other assessment tools, paint a more holistic picture of students' progress.
Assessment is separate from the curriculum and instruction; that is, there are special times, places and methods for assessment.	The lines between the curriculum and assessment are blurred; that is, assessment is always occurring in and through the curriculum and daily instruction.
Outside testing instruments and agents provide the only true and objective picture of student knowledge and learning.	The human factor, that is, people subjectively involved with students (for example, teachers, parents and the student themselves), holds the key to an accurate assessment process.

There is a clearly defined body of knowledge that students must master in school and be able to demonstrate or reproduce on a test.	Teaching students how to learn, how to think, and how to be intelligent in as many ways as possible (that is, creating lifelong learners) is the main goal of education.
If something can't be objectively tested in a uniform and standard way, it isn't worth teaching or learning.	The process of learning is as important as the content of the curriculum; not all learning can be objectively tested in a standardised manner.

So we are now dealing with a more complex process of assessment, because it must be suited/fitted to meet every unique individual.

A good starting point for assessing multiple intelligences is to use you own intuition and then make these conscious. Following that you do some observation of the child as they go about problem solving and creating. That way you will be able to focus the things you 'know' intuitively about a child, check them out against actual behavioural data (by observing) and then triangulate these two pieces of information with a conversation with the child to gain their own understanding of themselves too. Thus you end up with a multi process assessment, which captures a lot of lively data.

USING THE ASSESSMENTS:
Assessment of the different strengths a child uses is quite difficult and the best way to learn them is by close observation, using some of the characteristics of each style listed in this booklet as your guide. However we have found three other methods that give you a sound basis for forming an opinion about the particular MI profile of a child and these are shown in the following pages, where we have included photcopiable templates for use with your children.

1 Trust your instincts

2 Ask the children

3 Charting an MI Profile

MI ASSESSMENT 1 – TRUSTING YOUR INSTINCTS

Here is a template format for starting to make your intuitions conscious. It is followed by a semi-structured format for a discussion with a child about their own multiple intelligences:

MI ASSESSMENT 1
TRUSTING YOUR INSTINCTS

THE INFORMAL ASSESSMENT

When I think about _____(name) I recognise that the way he/she:

Likes to learn is by working with others and can really tune into other pupils' feelings and needs. (Interpersonal)	Y	N
Likes to learn is by reflecting and taking a bit of personal time to mull things over in relation to their own experience before commenting. (Intrapersonal)	Y	N
Likes to learn is by organising whatever he/she hears or sees into categories and sequences. Likes order around them. (Logical – mathematical intelligence)	Y	N
Likes to learn is by enjoying words, talking, reading and hearing a narrative rather than a lesson. (Linguistic)	Y	N
Likes to learn is when he/she is on the move and acting things out. (Kinaesthetic)	Y	N
Likes to learn is by seeing things in pictures and images. (Spatial)	Y	N
Likes to learn is by connecting what they are learning with sounds, music or rhythms. (Musical)	Y	N
Likes to learn things about natural world and how one thing affects another in nature. (Naturalist)	Y	N

MI ASSESSMENT 2
ASKING THE CHILDREN

QUESTION CHECKLIST

1 What do you enjoy doing?

....

2 Do you have any hobbies or games that you love playing?

....

3 What have you done that you feel proud of?

....

4 What does your friend/mother/teacher say you are good at?

....

5 If your friend was describing you what would they say?

....

6 How did you learn how to .... (favourite game/hobby/achievement)?

....

7 Which classes have you enjoyed?

....

8 If you think of a film you've seen recently, which part do you remember most easily – music, the story, the characters, the action, the sequence of events, the words, the costumes?

....

WORKSHEET

MI ASSESSMENT 3 – FOR CHILDREN
CHARTING THE MULTIPLE INTELLIGENCES

Here is a more comprehensive questionnaire to help you make your instinctive responses about a child more conscious. This can also be used with a child if you read it out to them and see what they think about their own tendencies as they tackle things and respond to the world. Even more information and interesting ways of working as a team emerge if you ask parents to become involved too. You will find templates for photocopying with slightly different phrasing for each party on pages 41-45.

Name.. Date....................

LINGUISTIC

I find it easy to memorise stories, poems, history facts and tidbits of information.	
I started to read relatively early.	
I write poems, notes and stories for fun.	
My parents say I was talkative from an early age.	
I love looking things up in reference books.	
I have a favourite story that they know off by heart.	
TOTAL	

LOGICAL - MATHEMATICAL

I like to mess around with experiments.	
I can always pick up a new numbers concept quickly.	
I like counting things.	
I ask questions about how things work and look for a cause and effect chain.	
I like programmes about science or numbers projects.	
I look for regularities and patterns in the world around me.	
TOTAL	

SPATIAL

I like to scribble and draw a lot.	
I find myself very drawn to certain colours.	
I like to put things back together again.	
I like to build card towers, sand castles and things that operate in 3D.	
I have vivid colourful dreams that I can remember.	
I can visualise things easily.	
I am good at finding my way around in the world.	
TOTAL	

MUSICAL

I like to bang, make noise and make rhythms.	
I love listening to tapes, music on the radio, and my favourite songs.	
I like to make up my own songs.	
I play a musical instrument and learn it easily.	
My mood changes when they hear music or a rhythmic beat.	
I have a good ear for different sounds and notice sounds that are going on around me.	
TOTAL	

BODILY - KINAESTHETIC

My parents/carers told me I started to walk/crawl early.	
I love finger painting, clay, play doh ® and other messy things.	
I am very physically active.	
I like messing around with little 'plays' or roleplays.	
I am good at particular sport.	
I love being outdoors.	
TOTAL	

INTRAPERSONAL

I am very independent.	
I have plenty of interests that take up all my time.	
I have a secret place.	
I think a lot about what I will do when I grow up.	
I like to discuss life's big issues.	
I have unusual spiritual/mystical experiences, for example in dreams, or when I visit certain places, that I seldom reveal to other people.	
I am very aware of my own separate identity.	
TOTAL	

INTERPERSONAL

I am friendly and feel confident around adults.	
I have plenty of friends at school.	
I am often called on to help friends out.	
I always know what's going on socially – who's having a party, who's planning a trip.	
I am usually invited to more social events than other children.	
I can tell what's going on between people when I walk into a room.	
I am caring with other people.	
TOTAL	

NATURALIST

I look for animal or bird tracks and know what made them.	
I like collecting natural objects.	
I love looking at natural objects.	
I am calm and sensitive to animals' needs so I am easily able to bond with pets.	
I really get into nature programmes on TV.	
I am conscious of the ecological impacts on nature made by man and care about this.	
TOTAL	

Complete the total scores on the histogram on the following page.

MY MULTIPLE INTELLIGENCE CHART

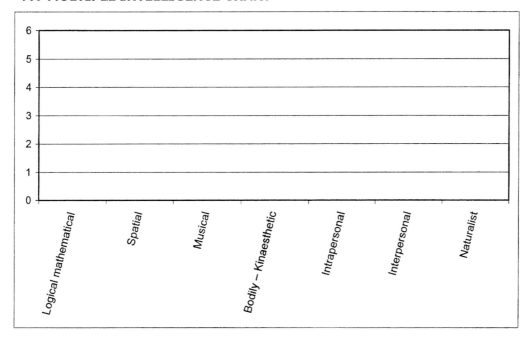

Think of yourself during a typical day and after reading through the prompts and ticking the ones that relate to you decide:

1 Which Multiple Intelligence you think you demonstrate most naturally?	
2 Which you demonstrate least comfortably?	
3 Place the rest in order of relative ease and ability.	__ Linguistic __ Logical mathematical __ Spatial __ Musical __ Bodily – Kinaesthetic __ Intrapersonal __ Interpersonal __ Naturalist

Remember that everyone will display all the intelligences and many actions you take will be combinations of several. Just notice which seems to be that bit more natural and easy for you and which you are less likely to go for.

W O R K S H E E T

4 DEVELOPING THE INTELLIGENCES IN YOUR CLASSROOM

EASY WAYS TO BEGIN

What follow are lists of ways to really use and develop the Multiple Intelligences each child has. To help yourself develop this differentiated approach to learning more clearly

- think of your lesson plans and see which methods you generally make use of.
- think of a child who may be struggling in the classroom and complete one of the previous assessments to see where their strengths may be.
- complete one for yourself as we all tend to teach to our own profile you may find you are building lesson plans that suit your particular style of learning.
- over a term complete a multiple intelligence assessment for all of the children either with them as part of a PSE lesson or on your own, or with colleagues and perhaps the parents.

Once you understand what is making everyone tick it should be easier to find ways to help everyone learn.

STRENGTHENING STRENGTHS – MAKING THE MOST OF WHAT YOU'VE GOT

One of the easiest and most positive ways to begin working with any individual or group is to work with what is already there and not causing too much of a problem. Here I am calling that 'strengthening strengths'. One of the main

problems with the old paradigms of assessment and intelligence are that they have been used as a way of thinking about the deficits in the child. What have they not got, what are their weaknesses, what needs to be remedied? This way, by taking the strengths, we are looking at things quite differently. We are already changing our focus and looking for what is

working and celebrating that. It is like working with the river. If we want to make life easy for ourselves we will design things so that we use the power and energy of the river's natural flow to carry timber, boats, people etc downstream. Thus using the least amount of energy and getting the fastest performance. If we tried to send goods upstream against the flow think how much harder that would be. The same principle applies here. This means that it will make life easier for everyone if you teach things in the following formats for children who already have a strong penchant for that method. Later deficits and weaknesses can be considered but only once the strengths have really been maximised.

LINGUISTIC

1. Being involved in a reading group
2. Dictating into tape recorder
3. Writing reports after doing desk research
4. Doing work sheets
5. Hearing information being given out
6. Surfing the net
7. Using a dictionary
8. Using mnemonics to remember things by
9. Doing an outline of a story
10. Summarising the main points of a lesson
11. Writing letters to friends telling them what they have learnt
12. Reading

LOGICAL – MATHEMATICAL

1. Brainstorming ideas then organising them into a sequence
2. Calculating
3. Collecting data
4. Drawing up tables and frequency charts
5. Creating a time line
6. Making a flow diagram of a problem
7. Dividing the lesson into parts
8. Having an agenda to follow
9. Making lists
10. Ticking things off
11. Using numbers as memory triggers

SPATIAL

1. Making a cartoon of the subject
2. Colour coding aspects of the lesson
3. Making a story board
4. Doodling
5. Finding pictures related to the content of lesson and describing them
6. Getting an overview
7. Playing Pictionary
8. Seeing maps and following them
9. Seeing textures
10. Using graphics software
11. Watching a video

MUSICAL

1. Associating learning with sounds
2. Finding songs that have relevant lyrics
3. Rhyming
4. Singing
5. Learning while listening to music
6. Reading aloud to a beat
7. Making rap songs up
8. Humming
9. Listening
10. Tape recording self reading and then listening to tape

BODILY – KINAESTHETIC

1. Being an apprentice
2. Doing body sculpts
3. Creating drama projects
4. Exercising while thinking things through
5. Having a squeeze ball to mess with while learning
6. Learning about sports heroes and heroines
7. Miming
8. Practising something many times
9. Taking field trips
10. Walking and reading at same time
11. Writing ideas on cards so that they can be manipulated

INTRAPERSONAL

1. Thinking through something alone before sharing
2. Having own project to complete
3. Keeping a diary
4. Reading
5. Researching
6. Mapping out possibilities
7. Making up theories and hypotheses
8. Writing a summary of the class activities and main learning points
9. Making connections and patterns between things
10. Questioning

INTERPERSONAL

1. Acting out what is learned
2. Talking to peers to get ideas to bounce off
3. Asking questions
4. Be encouraged for talking and asking
5. Brainstorming
6. Having a buddy/mentor/classroom coach
7. Debating
8. Having a friendly relationship with teacher
9. Imagination and empathy
10. Interviewing
11. Listening to other people's experiences
12. Participating in group or community work
13. Role playing
14. Teaching someone else

NATURALIST

1. Observing things through their senses such as touching, listening, smelling
2. Grouping natural objects into categories
3. Doing field studies outside
4. Having responsibility for class/school animals
5. Having projects where they photograph, draw or video a natural phenomenon
6. Set up a recycling project
7. Designing experiments
8. Identifying natural sounds
9. Watching nature films and answering category and observation questions afterwards
10. Performing roleplays of animal behaviour

TECHNIQUES YOU CAN TEACH STUDENTS TO USE WHEN THEY ARE FEELING FRUSTRATED

Not every teacher or adult a child comes into contact with will know about Multiple Intelligences and how each child has a different profile of intelligences that help them feel good and effective when they use them as channels to learn things. This can often lead to the students getting bored and frustrated when they are being asked to tackle things in ways that just don't add up for them. If you teach them about their MI's and then show them how they can take some control over their own learning process once they leave the class (or even when they are in it) this will help them a lot.   These can be given to a student when they are going to lessons they have a negative history about. If they remind themselves of ways to help make sense of what they hear then that may make them more empowered and attentive. They need to know that humans are fallible and sometimes they need to be more creative than the teacher they are with at that time.

Linguistic	• Read a story • Talk to self into a tape recorder • Write a diary entry • Email a friend telling them what has happened
Logical mathematical	• Count to 10 • Doing some arithmetic problems • Make a list of events • Make a time line of the situation
Spatial	• Draw pictures of how feels • Visualise a peaceful setting • Do some art therapy • Create a collage or patchwork • Imagine body into a calm state
Musical	• Find a musical mentor • Do a music inventory for the class • Be allocated responsibility for music related tasks • Listen to a tape • Research something about music • Reward self with some music

Bodily Kinaesthetic	• Do something that uses body like being a playground monitor, setting up the room for next class, clearing the garage.
	• Do some exercises before next activity
	• Get a game set up on the Gameboy ® to have as a reward once next activity completed
	• Sit at the end of the table so that can wriggle without disturbing the others
Intrapersonal	• Make a plan to stop the situation from happening again
	• Find out how they are feeling by listening to own body language
	• Write in journal
	• Find a quiet spot to think in
Interpersonal	• Call home or a friend
	• Imagine how someone else might handle the situation
	• Ask friend to come round
	• Read a story about someone with a similar problem
Naturalist	• Imagine themselves in a favourite spot in nature
	• See how many objects in the room are made of natural substances
	• Notice how many blue, green, brown things there are in the room
	• Guess how long it will take to finish what you are doing
	• Find a natural metaphor for the situation that is frustrating you, think how nature solves the problem.

5 WAYS TO BUILD EACH DIFFERENT INTELLIGENCE

Everybody has all these Intelligences to a greater or lesser extent and we all use them all the time so there will always be something to build on whatever area you or the student want to develop.

As a rule of thumb you need to teach something new to a child using their learning strengths. Thus if you are introducing a new concept in your maths lesson and you know that most of your students have a strength in their kinaesthetic intelligence you would make sure to deliver the topic in very movement oriented ways. Thereafter you could teach extensions and repetitions of the concept in other styles to stretch and expand your learners. Once students know something about the concept (though their preferred style) it is much easier for them to pick up extension information about it through their other multiple intelligences.

With this in mind it is helpful once you have completed everyone's MI assessment to do a little more arithmetic and work out the proportions of the class who have strengths in certain areas. We already know that the majority of children, in particular boys, will be kinaesthetic. Thus it makes sense to present many of your learning concepts in this format. They can then be backed up by repetitions in other formats to keep building flexibility.

BUILDING UP WEAKER AREAS

This is where 'stretching' comes in – children need a moderate degree of stress to help their brains develop strongly and creatively. Thus it is helpful to keep making the material available to them in all the different formats. They will start to strengthen the areas that have not been so well used before. The brain is like a muscle – if you use it and stretch it in steady regular sessions it will strengthen and develop.

Linguistic	1	play word games with friends and family
	2	go to a creative writing class
	3	find a magazine about something you are really interested in a read it regularly
	4	read to/teach or mentor a younger child
	5	go to the local bookshop/library when they are having a storytelling event.
Logical-mathematical	1	play Logical-mathematical games with friends and family (Go, Clue, dominoes)
	2	work on a book of puzzles
	3	read about a famous mathematician or scientist
	4	watch documentaries about science subjects
	5	visit the Planetarium or science museum
Spatial	1	work on Rubiks cube, mazes or other visual puzzles
	2	use a camcorder and learn how to create good short clips
	3	plan and design decoration for your room
	4	look for images and pictures in cloud shapes, cracks the wall etc
	5	rent 'how to' videos on subjects you are interested in
Musical	1	sing or hum in the shower
	2	play name that tune with friends and family
	3	spend a bit of time each week listening to different forms and styles of music, notice what you prefer or dislike.
	4	Read music critiques in the papers
	5	Find a way to play music on the computer.

Bodily Kinaesthetic	1	join a sports club
	2	learn a craft
	3	play video games that need quick reflexes
	4	develop hand eye coordination by juggling balls
	5	learn to type since it requires dexterity
Intrapersonal	1	learn to meditate
	2	learn a form of moving meditation such as tai chi
	3	read self-help books
	4	write your own autobiography
	5	find out what you really enjoy doing and make sure that you give yourself this treat regularly
Interpersonal	1	decide to meet one new person every week
	2	fill a diary with names and contact details of friends, family and acquaintances and contact one or two every week by phone, email, in person or letter
	3	join a volunteer group such as Red Cross, scouts etc
	4	find a person who displays this intelligence and ask them to be your mentor or offer to be a mentor for someone else.
	5	smile at everyone you meet.
Naturalist	1	visit a zoo
	2	have a bird feeding table in the garden/play area and be responsible for having food on it
	3	take regular walks and notice whether you prefer woods, seaside, wetlands, town parks....
	4	grow simple plants such as mustard and cress
	5	play around with microscopes and describe what you see

5 THE MULTIPLE INTELLIGENCE ENVIRONMENT

Many schools and classrooms favour the linguistic and mathematical intelligences – back to the influence of the old paradigms again! However paying attention to the other intelligences and how they can be stimulated is also important to consider in the classroom and school environment.

DIFFERENT LOCATIONS

Think about each location and see what you are doing already towards making the school an MI friendly zone for the students in your school.

	Playground	Classroom	Corridors	Offices
Linguistic				
Logical - Mathematical				
Spatial				
Musical				
Bodily-Kinaesthetic				
Intrapersonal				
Interpersonal				
Naturalist				

Please see the template overleaf for an example of the grids to use, for full observation grids see CD in the back of this book. Putting in ticks/crosses/notes etc in 'handwriting' text.

For example:

Linguistic	Playground	Classroom	Corridors	Offices
Vocabulary expanding words on the walls	x	✓	✓	x
Playground may be difficult to have words around, more classrooms need to have words on wall. Must speak to all staff members at meeting! Make a list of vocabulary words				
Written signs to direct people	✓	✓	✓	✓
Could do with making these signs more interesting and maybe having a school map around the school				

MATERIALS YOU CAN HAVE AVAILABLE IN YOUR CLASSROOM

Linguistic
WP programmes
Tape recorder
Reading library
Calligraphy set
Email facility
Wordsearch puzzles

Logical mathematical
Science kits
Calculator
Monopoly
Card games
Clock
Access/Excel type software

Spatial
Maps
Camcorder
Telescope/microscope
Night vision goggles
Drawing/painting equipment
Cartoon books
Collage material
Software to design gardens/spaces/interiors

Musical
Recordings
Instruments
Singing games
Radio
Data streaming facility on PC
Sound boxes with mystery sounds

Bodily kinaesthetic
Toolbox
Building games – Lego, Duplex
Play doh ®
Model kits
Masks
Sports equipment
Boxes, cardboard rolls, containers
Machines to take apart and repair/tinker with

Intrapersonal
Make up kit
Empty journals/diaries
Cards
Solitaire
Reference library
Access to internet

Interpersonal
Party supplies
Internet connection
Access to discussion groups and forums
Board games for groups to play

Naturalist
Collectors kit
Magnifying glass
Binoculars
Ant farm/worm farm
Garden equipment
Aquarium

6 WHAT NEXT

One of the most important ways that you can help learners learn through using this knowledge about their Multiple Intelligences is through knowing your own particular profile too. It stands to reason that if you are strong on Musical and Linguistic Intelligences that you will tend to major on them as ways of conveying information in your classroom. This isn't wrong – just a point worth noting. It may then be helpful for you to think about how some of the students you struggle with like to learn – what is their MI profile like – and is it very like yours or very different? In my case I work more easily with children who have a similar profile to mine. It gives me a short cut to their minds and makes my life easier, which means that I have more energy and therefore more enthusiasm. A nice positive cycle is established. However a friend of mine works very well with pupils who have a very different profile to hers. She likes the challenge and finds that she is expanding her repertoire of ways to teach through her own learning. Sticking with her own styles is boring!

My own particular interest is in Emotional Intelligence, and its practical correlate, Emotional Literacy. I think that the personal intelligences are ones that we all of us need to be really skilled in no matter what job we may need up doing. Unless we are a hermit we are going to need interpersonal abilities and unless someone else regulates all aspects of our life we need intrapersonal intelligence to help us manage ourselves happily and effectively. I also think that skills in these areas tend to support our effective learning and success in the others. The personal intelligences are another area where the self-awareness and amount of modelling a teacher, or parent does, is crucial to imparting the skills to children. You have to begin with yourself, and from that a deeper understanding and capacity to influence your students and children emerges.

Undertaking one of the Continuing Professional Development courses in Emotional Literacy, which covers Multiple Intelligences too, is a way that you can combine personal development with professional applications and win in both dimensions. Further details about these courses are available by visiting www.schoolofemotional-literacy.com

YOU AND YOUR MULTIPLE INTELLIGENCE PROFILE

Linguistic

Books are important to me.	
I hear words in my head before I read, speak, or write.	
I get more out of listening to the radio or a cassette than watching a video or the TV.	
I have aptitude for games like scrabble, anagrams, and passwords.	
I enjoy tongue twisters, puns etc.	
I am sometimes asked to explain the meaning of words.	
English, social studies, and history are easier for me than maths and science.	
I pay more attention to words on adverts as I travel through the town centre than buildings or environment.	
Conversation often refers to things I have heard or read.	
I have written something recently or spoken on a subject that received good attention.	
TOTAL	/10

Logical mathematical

I can compute numbers in my head.	
I play games and teasers that involve logical deduction or sequencing.	
I like to set up little experiments – if I double the amount of plant food I give what will be the result?	
My mind searches for patterns, regularities, logical sequences in things.	
I am interested in new developments in science.	
I believe that most things have a have rational explanation.	
I think in wordless, abstract concepts, often without images to go with them.	
I find logical flaws in things other people have said or done.	
I feel more comfortable once things have been measured, categorised, analysed, and quantified in some way.	
TOTAL	/9

Spatial

I see clear visual images when I close my eyes.	
I like using a camera or camcorder to record what is going on.	
I enjoy jigsaws, mosaics, mazes and other visual puzzles.	
I have vivid dreams quite often.	
I can generally find my way around unfamiliar territory.	
I like to draw or doodle.	
I find geometry easier than algebra.	
I can easily imagine how something would look if seen from a bird's eye perspective.	
I like looking at reading matter that is heavily illustrated.	
TOTAL	/9

Musical

I have a pleasant talking voice.	
I can tell when a note is off key.	
I frequently listen to music on the radio, cassette etc.	
I play a musical instrument.	
My life would be poorer without sounds and rhythm around.	
I find myself walking around with a TV jingle or tune running through my head.	
I can easily keep time clapping or tapping to a piece of music.	
I know tunes to a lot of different songs or pieces.	
If I hear a rhythm/song/musical piece I can reproduce it fairly accurately.	
I often make little tapping routines or hums while working, studying or learning something new.	
TOTAL	/10

WORKSHEET

Bodily - Kinaesthetic

I engage in some sport activity regularly.	
I find it difficult to sit still for long periods of time.	
I like working at concrete activities with my hands eg weaving, sewing, modelling, mechanics.	
My best ideas come when involved in some physical activity – walking, jogging, swimming.	
I frequently use hand gestures when conversing with others.	
I need to touch things to learn more about them.	
I enjoy dare-devil amusement rides or thrilling physical challenges.	
I would describe myself as well-coordinated.	
I need to practice new skills rather than see them demonstrated.	
TOTAL	/9

Intrapersonal

I regularly spend time reflecting, thinking, meditating, wondering about important life questions.	
I have attended counselling or personal growth sessions of some sort to learn more about myself.	
I read self-help books for the same reason.	
I have my own opinions.	
I have a special interest or hobby that I keep private.	
I have important goals for my life that I think about on a regular basis.	
I have a realistic view of myself that I have found out through feedback and reflection.	
I would rather be in a quiet cabin in the woods than a busy entertaining resort.	
I am often considered to be strong willed/independent minded.	
I often keep a journal to keep me in touch with the events of me inner life, such as my dreams and my emotional responses to places and people.	
I am self-employed or very autonomous in work or have thought a lot about starting my own business.	
TOTAL	/11

WORKSHEET

Interpersonal

People come to me for advice or suggestions about their situation.	
I prefer team sports to individual ones such as swimming.	
I like to talk problems through rather than mull over them alone.	
I have at least three close friends.	
I like games like Monopoly, bridge rather than crosswords or individual computer games.	
I like to teach someone else what I know how to do.	
I am often considered as the leader in a group.	
I feel comfortable in a crowd.	
I like to get involved in community/social activities.	
I would rather spend an evening at a lively social gathering than at home alone.	
TOTAL	/10

Naturalist

I have always enjoyed the outdoors.	
I have hobbies such as hiking, fishing, rock climbing.	
I am very conscious of smells and natural sounds where-ever I go.	
I regularly retreat to natural spaces to revitalise.	
I have got green fingers.	
I always had a pet or an ongoing relationship with some animals.	
I collect or collected minerals, flowers, insects etc (and often still have these collections).	
I am comfortable rooting around in mulch or 'yucky' material when exploring.	
I am very good at spotting even the smallest detail.	
I feel an affinity for the natural world.	
I get excited about a flower coming into bloom or the return of the swallows.	
TOTAL	/11

Complete totals on the histogram over the page.

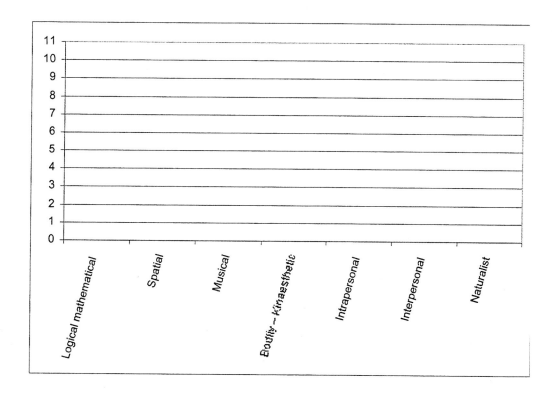

What does this mean about how you teach?

_____

_____

_____

Think of a lesson plan that you were planning to use this week and do the Multiple Intelligence test on it.

Now turn to the Action Plan page and make some notes or mind maps for yourself as you plan the next steps to integrating multiple intelligences into your classroom

MI ASSESSMENT 3 – FOR PARENTS/CARERS
CHARTING THE MULTIPLE INTELLIGENCES

Child's name.................................. Date......................

LINGUISTIC

He/she finds it easy to memorise stories, poems, history facts and tidbits of information.	
She/he started to read relatively early.	
He/she writes poems, notes and stories for fun.	
She/he was talkative from an early age.	
He/she loves looking things up in reference books.	
I have a favourite story that they know off by heart.	
She/he has favourite stories that they know off by heart.	
TOTAL	

LOGICAL - MATHEMATICAL

She/he likes messing around with experiments.	
He/she can always pick up a new numbers concept quickly.	
She/he likes counting things.	
He/she asks questions about how things work and looks for a cause and effect chain.	
She/he likes programmes about science or numbers projects.	
He/she looks for regularities and patterns in the world around them.	
TOTAL	

WORKSHEET

SPATIAL

She/he scribbles and draws a lot.	
He/she is very drawn to certain colours.	
She/he likes to put things back together again.	
He/she likes building card towers, sand castles and things that operate in 3D.	
She/he has vivid colourful dreams that they can remember.	
He/she can visualise things easily.	
She/he is good at finding their way around in the world.	
TOTAL	

MUSICAL

She/he likes to bang, make noise and make rhythms.	
He/she loves listening to tapes, music on the radio, and their favourite songs.	
She/he likes to make up their own songs.	
He/she plays a musical instrument and learns it easily.	
Her/his mood changes when they hear music or a rhythmic beat.	
He/she has a good ear for different sounds and notices what is going on around them aurally.	
TOTAL	

WORKSHEET

BODILY - KINAESTHETIC

She/he was early to walk/crawl.	
He/she loves finger painting, clay, play doh ® and other messy things.	
She/he is very physically active.	
He/she likes messing around with little 'playlets' or roleplays.	
She/he is good at particular sports.	
He/she loves being out doors.	
TOTAL	

INTRAPERSONAL

She/he is very self-reliant and independent.	
He/she has plenty of interests that take up their time alone.	
She/he has a secret place.	
He/she is very thoughtful about what they will do when they grow up.	
She/he is reflective about life's big issues and will ask profound questions.	
He/she has unusual, spiritual/mystic experiences that they seldom reveal.	
She/he is very aware of their own identity.	
TOTAL	

WORKSHEET

INTERPERSONAL

She/he is friendly and confident with adults.	
He/she has plenty of friends at school.	
She/he is often called on to help friends out.	
He/she always knows what's going on socially – who's having a party etc	
She/he is usually invited to more social events than other children.	
He/she can tell what's going on between people when they walk into a room.	
She/he is compassionate and caring with other people.	
TOTAL	

NATURALIST

She/he looks for animal or bird tracks and knows what made them.	
He/she likes collecting natural objects.	
She/he loves looking at natural phenomena.	
He/she is calm and sensitive to animals needs so is able to bond with pets easily.	
She/he really gets engrossed when there is a nature programme on TV.	
He/she is conscious of ecological impacts made by man and sensitive about this.	
TOTAL	

Think of the child during a typical day and after reading through the prompts decide:

1 Which Multiple Intelligence do you think they demonstrate most naturally?	
2 Which do they demonstrate with least comfort and ability?	
3 Place the rest in order of relative ease and ability.	__ Linguistic __ Logical mathematical __ Spatial __ Musical __ Bodily – Kinaesthetic __ Intrapersonal __ Interpersonal __ Naturalist

Remember that each child will display all the intelligences and many actions you take will be combinations of several. Just notice which seems to be that bit more natural and easy for them and which they are less likely to go for.

Action Plan

....

....

....

....

....

....

....

....

....

....

....

....

....

....

....

....

....

....

W O R K S H E E T

School of Emotional Literacy

The School of Emotional Literacy was created to provide on-going professional training in emotional literacy development. It enables people to train as specialists in emotional literacy assessment and development who are then well qualified to provide consultancy and training in this subject to schools, LEAs, social services and community education services.

School Principal, Dr Elizabeth Morris, is a psychologist, psychotherapist and trainer who has specialised in the assessment and development of emotional literacy and self-esteem for the last twenty three years. She set up the online Self Esteem Advisory Service in response to the increasing demand for information on the topic and has developed the Self-Esteem Indicator as a diagnostic tool for assessing pupil's self esteem. This has been published by NFER-Nelson. She writes extensively on the subjects of self-esteem and emotional literacy.

The School of Emotional Literacy runs a Post Graduate Certificate and an Advanced Diploma in Emotional Literacy Development at Bristol University for any professional working with young people or families. The programme is also available at other centres throughout the UK such as Edinburgh, Glasgow, London & West Midlands. The University of Bristol also runs the School's programmes on emotional intelligence and self-motivation, emotional coaching and self esteem building. These courses are attended by parents as well as educators. A distance learning and tutor contact Certificate is now in development.

Training and Inset Workshops

The School of Emotional Literacy offers a number of courses related to self-esteem, emotional literacy and brain-based learning and welcomes anyone interested in the development of children, pupils and young people to their training days and workshops.

Topics include:
- Introducing emotional literacy - releasing the potential in your school
- Puppets, play and poetry
- The emotionally literate approach to anger management
- In what ways is that child intelligent
- Building self-esteem in classrooms
- The emotionally literate approach to behaviour management

For a full training list and further information, please visit www.schoolofemotional-literacy.com

Other Publications

1. The Whole School Emotional Literacy Indicator by Elizabeth Morris and Caroline Scott
2. The Class Emotional Literacy Indicator by Elizabeth Morris and Caroline Scott
3. The Individual Emotional Literacy Indicator by Elizabeth Morris and Caroline Scott
4. Developing Social Skills – A Practical Solution by Elizabeth Scott
5. Build Self-esteem first – A Practical Solution by Athy Demitriades
6. Establishing a Counselling Service in your School – A Practical Solution by Emma Wills
7. I feel.... when..... Posters developed by Elizabeth Morris
8. Graffiti Feelings Posters
9. Bullies aren't bad. An emotionally literate response to bullying   by Heather Jenkins
10. 'SISTERS' Club Facilitators File by Annie Hamlaoui
11. Emotional Resilience Profile by Elizabeth Morris
12. Self Esteem Guidelines: developing a whole school policy by Elizabeth Morris
13. Face your Feelings Game by Liz Tew and James Bocot
14. Feelings Game by Heather Jenkins
15. IT'S OKAY TO BE ME by Annie Hamlaoui
16. How does it feel? An Emotional Literacy Programme for pupils at risk of exclusion or following PEX by Susie Davis
17. The School and it's Counselling Service - a companion guide to "Establishing a Counselling Service in Your School -A Practical Guide" by Emma Wills
18. Multiple Intelligences in the Classroom: At-a-glance Guide to Assessing and Teaching using Multiple Intelligence Theory by Elizabeth Morris
19. Emotional Literacy Indicator for Early Years by Elizabeth Morris and Caroline Scott
20. More than 40 ways to develop emotional literacy in pupils by Elizabeth Morris

Bibliography

Arnold E. (1999) The MI Strategy Bank, Zephyr Press

Damasio A. (1999) The feeling of what happens: body and emotion in the making of consciousness, Harcourt Brace

Elias M. Tobias S. Friedlander B. & Goleman D. (1999) Emotionally intelligence parenting, Hodder and Stoughton

Gardner H. (1999) Intelligence reframed: multiple intelligences for the 20th century, Basic Books

Gardner H. (1993) Frames of Mind: The Theory of Multiple Intelligences, Fontana Press

Gardner H. (1993) Multiple Intelligences, Basic Books

Goleman D. (1996) Emotional Intelligence, Bloomsbury

Gottman J. (1997) The Heart of Parenting: How to raise an emotionally intelligence child, Bloomsbury

Jensen E. (1995) The learning brain, Turning Point Publications

Kagan S and M. (1998) Multiple Intelligences: the complete MI book, Kagan Cooperative Learning

LeDoux J. (1998) The emotional brain: the mysterious underpinnings of emotional life, Simon & Schuster Inc

Morris E. (2002) Insight: Assessing and Developing Self-Esteem, NferNelson

Morris E. (2003) Assertiveness Programme, Incentive Publishing

Morris E. (2002) Anger Management Programme, Incentive Publishing

Morris E & K. (2002) The Powerhouse: An all-in-one resource for building self esteem in primary schools, Lucky Duck Publishing

Nelson K. (1998) Developing Students' Multiple Intelligences: Hundreds of Practical Ideas Easily Integrated Into Your Lessons and Activities

Promislow S. (2000) Making The Brain Body Connection, Access Publishers Network

Thomas A. (1999) Seven Kinds of Smart, Plume Publishing

Thomas A. (2000) In Their Own Way: Discovering and Encouraging Your Child's Multiple Intelligences, G P Putnam's Sons

Multiple Intelligences in the Classroom

At-A-Glance Guide to Assessing and Teaching using Multiple Intelligence Theory

Dr Elizabeth Morris